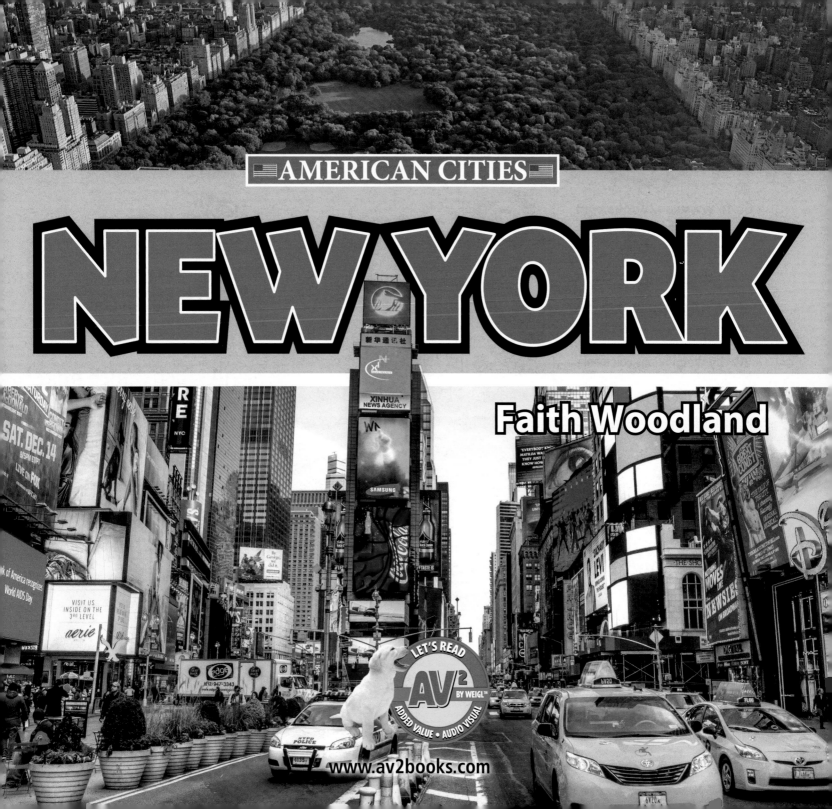

AMERICAN CITIES

NEW YORK

Faith Woodland

LET'S READ
AV²
BY WEIGL™
ADDED VALUE • AUDIO VISUAL

Go to **www.av2books.com**, and enter this book's unique code.

BOOK CODE

AVP34822

AV² by Weigl brings you media enhanced books that support active learning.

AV² provides enriched content that supplements and complements this book. Weigl's AV² books strive to create inspired learning and engage young minds in a total learning experience.

Your AV² Media Enhanced books come alive with...

Audio
Listen to sections of the book read aloud.

Video
Watch informative video clips.

Embedded Weblinks
Gain additional information for research.

Try This!
Complete activities and hands-on experiments.

Key Words
Study vocabulary, and complete a matching word activity.

Quizzes
Test your knowledge.

Slide Show
View images and captions, and prepare a presentation.

... and much, much more!

Published by AV² by Weigl
350 5th Avenue, 59th Floor   New York, NY 10118
Website: www.av2books.com

Library of Congress Cataloging-in-Publication Data

Names: Woodland, Faith, author.
Title: New York / Faith Woodland.
Description: New York, NY : AV2 by Weigl, 2018. I Series: American cities
Identifiers: LCCN 2017049438 (print) I LCCN 2017049815 (ebook) I ISBN
  9781489673060 (Multi User ebook) I ISBN 9781489673053 (hardcover) I
ISBN 9781489677624 (softcover)
Subjects: LCSH: New York (N.Y.)--Juvenile literature. I New York
  (N.Y.)--Guidebooks--Juvenile literature.
Classification: LCC F128.33 (ebook) I LCC F128.33 .W66 2018 (print) I DDC
  974.7/1--dc23
LC record available at https://lccn.loc.gov/2017049438

Printed in the United States of America in Brainerd, Minnesota
1 2 3 4 5 6 7 8 9 0   22 21 20 19 18

032018
150318

Editor: Heather Kissock   Designer: Ana María Vidal

Weigl acknowledges Getty Images, Alamy, Shutterstock, and iStock as the primary image suppliers for this title.

Contents

3

Get to Know New York

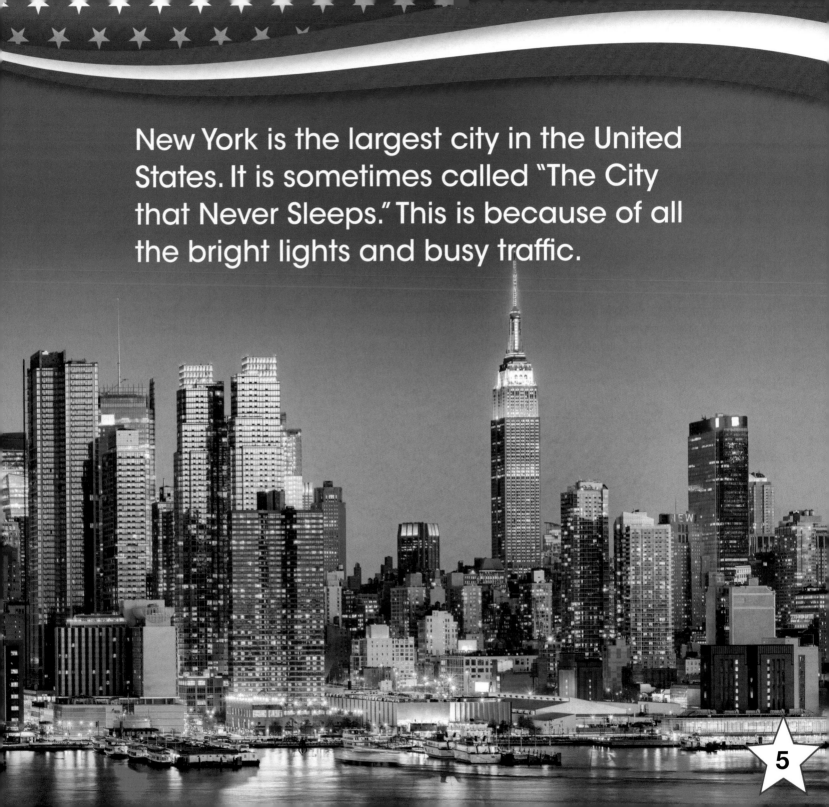

New York is the largest city in the United States. It is sometimes called "The City that Never Sleeps." This is because of all the bright lights and busy traffic.

Map of New York State

United States Map

New York

Alaska Hawai'i

MAP LEGEND

☆ New York City
● Capital City
▮ New York State
▮ United States
▮ Canada
▯ Water

SCALE
0 — 35 Miles

N

VERMONT

Adirondack Mountains

Fort Ticonderoga

NEW HAMPSHIRE

Lake Ontario

Baseball Hall of Fame, Cooperstown

● **ALBANY**

MASSACHUSETTS

NEW YORK

Niagara Falls

Lake Erie

CONNECTICUT

PENNSYLVANIA

NEW JERSEY

NEW YORK CITY ☆

Atlantic Ocean

Where Is New York?

New York City is in the southeast corner of New York State. It is about 150 miles south of the state's capital city, Albany. You can get there from New York City by driving on the I-87 highway.

There are many other places to visit in New York State. You can use a road map to plan a trip. Which roads could you take from New York City to these other places? How long might it take you to get to each place?

TRAVELING NEW YORK STATE
New York City to the Adirondack Mountains 273 miles
New York City to Fort Ticonderoga 266 miles
New York City to Cooperstown 199 miles
New York City to Niagara Falls 396 miles

Climate

New York City has a humid, or moist, climate. Spring is warm, and summer is hot. Rainfall helps flowers grow and grass become green.

Fall is cool and crisp. Winter brings cold temperatures and snow. The city gets about 2 feet of snow every year.

Summer temperatures in New York City can be as high as **106° Fahrenheit**.

Population and Geography

More than 8.5 million people live in New York City. Houses and apartments are often built close together. The city can be quite crowded at times.

New York City is found where the Hudson River meets the Atlantic Ocean. Much of the city sits on three islands. Bridges were built to link the islands to each other.

Many Peoples

Aboriginal Peoples lived in the New York City area long before anyone else. They hunted on the land and fished in the rivers. Later, people from Europe arrived. They began building settlements. Over time, the city of New York grew.

Today, New York City is home to people from all over the world. As many as 800 different languages are spoken in the city.

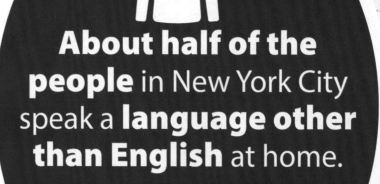

About half of the people in New York City speak a **language other than English** at home.

Tourism

Millions of people visit New York City every year. Many come to see the Empire State Building. They can take an elevator up 102 floors to get great views of the city.

New York is also known for its world-class theaters. Most are found along a street called Broadway. Visitors come to Broadway to see the latest plays and musicals.

The Empire State Building has **73 elevators**. They move at a speed of **1,400 feet** per **second**.

Sports

New York City is home to many major sports teams. The Yankees and the Mets play baseball. The Giants and the Jets are the city's main football teams.

The Rangers and the Islanders play hockey for the city. The Knicks and the Brooklyn Nets are the city's major basketball teams.

Economy

New York City is a center for business. Much of this business takes place on and around Wall Street. Many banks and other companies have their main offices in the city.

The city's port is busy all year. Ships arrive at the port with goods to sell. They also take goods made in the United States to other countries.

1 mile

Wall Street is **less** than **1/2 of a mile** long.

19

New York Timeline

10,000 years ago
Aboriginal Peoples hunt, fish, and farm in the New York City area.

1524
An explorer named Giovanni da Verrazzano becomes the first European to sail into New York Bay.

1625
The Dutch build a settlement in the area. It is called New Amsterdam.

1664
The British take over New Amsterdam and rename it New York.

1785
New York City becomes the nation's first capital city. It remains the capital until 1790.

2001
Terrorists fly two airliners into New York's World Trade Center.

1886
The Statue of Liberty is unveiled in New York Harbor.

2016
The new World Trade Center's Transportation Hub opens.

Things to Do in New York

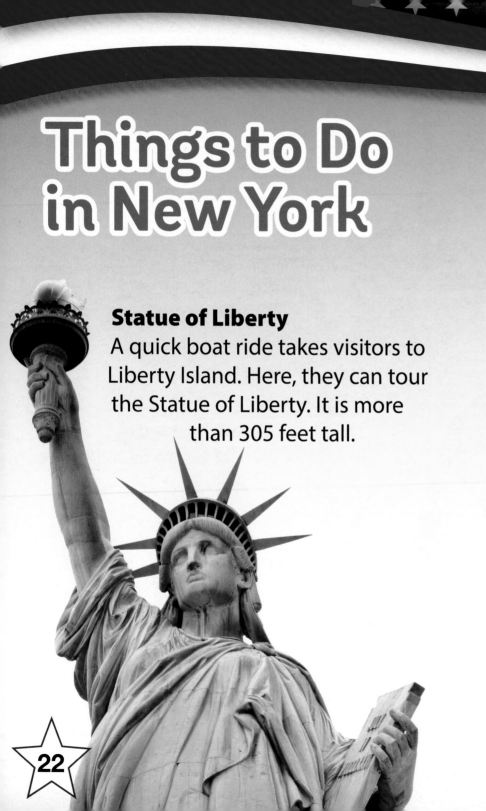

Statue of Liberty
A quick boat ride takes visitors to Liberty Island. Here, they can tour the Statue of Liberty. It is more than 305 feet tall.

One World Trade Center
One World Trade Center is New York's tallest building. People can visit floors 100, 101, and 102 to look out over the city.

Central Park

Central Park has 843 acres of green space. Besides gardens and lakes, the park also includes ball fields, an outdoor theater, and a zoo.

Brooklyn Bridge

This bridge has linked the community of Brooklyn to Manhattan Island for more than 135 years.

Times Square

People visit Times Square to see the bright lights of the square's many billboards.

23

KEY WORDS

Research has shown that as much as 65 percent of all written material published in English is made up of 300 words. These 300 words cannot be taught using pictures or learned by sounding them out. They must be recognized by sight. This book contains 107 common sight words to help young readers improve their reading fluency and comprehension. This book also teaches young readers several important content words, such as proper nouns. These words are paired with pictures to aid in learning and improve understanding.

Page	Sight Words First Appearance
4	get, know, to
5	all, and, because, city, in, is, it, lights, never, of, sometimes, states, that, the, this
7	a, about, are, by, can, could, each, how, from, long, many, might, miles, on, other, places, take, there, these, use, where, which, you
8	as, be, every, feet, grow, has, helps, high, or, year
11	at, close, found, houses, live, more, much, often, people, than, three, times, together, were
12	before, began, different, home, land, later, over, rivers, they, world
15	along, also, an, come, for, great, its, most, move, plays, second, see, up
19	around, goods, have, made, their, with
20	farm, first, into, named
21	opens, two, until
22	do, here, look, one, out, things

Page	Content Words First Appearance
4	New York
5	traffic, United States
7	Albany, highway, map, roads, trip
8	climate, fall, flowers, grass, rainfall, snow, spring, summer, temperatures, winter
11	apartments, Atlantic Ocean, bridges, geography, Hudson River, islands, population
12	Aboriginal Peoples, area, English, Europe, languages, settlements
15	Broadway, elevator, Empire State Building, floors, musicals, street, theaters, tourism, visitors
16	baseball, Brooklyn Nets, Giants, hockey, Islanders, Jets, Knicks, Mets, Rangers, sports, teams, Yankees
19	banks, business, center, companies, countries, economy, offices, port, ships, Wall Street
20	British, Dutch, explorer, Giovanni da Verrazzano, New Amsterdam, New York Bay, timeline
21	airliners, New York Harbor, Statue of Liberty, terrorists, Transportation Hub, World Trade Center
22	Liberty Island
23	ball fields, billboards, Brooklyn Bridge, Central Park, community, gardens, green space, lakes, Manhattan Island, Times Square, zoo